LIVE
WORTHY
OF THE
GOSPEL

LIFETOUCH SERIES

Walking in the Spirit: A Study Through Galatians 5
Run the Race: A Study Through Hebrews 12
Wisdom from Above: A Study in James
Live Worthy of the Gospel: A Study in Philippians

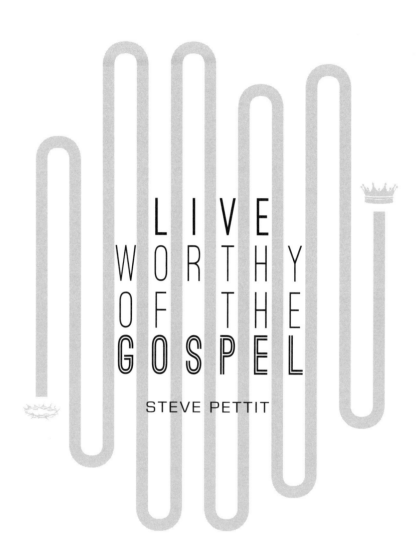

LIVE WORTHY OF THE GOSPEL

STEVE PETTIT

journeyforth®

Greenville, South Carolina

Photo Credit: Steve Pettit © 2014, Hal Cook, BJU Photo Services

Live Worthy of the Gospel: A Study in Philippians
Steve Pettit

Contributor: Eric Newton
Art Director: Elly Kalagayan
Designer: NaEun Hyun
Page Layout: by Michael Boone

© 2016 by BJU Press
Greenville, South Carolina 29614
JourneyForth Books is a division of BJU Press.

Printed in the United States of America

ISBN 978-1-62856-062-6

15   14   13   12   11   10   9   8   7   6   5   4   3   2   1

I dedicate this study to my wife of thirty-five years, Terry,
who has lived worthy of the gospel as long as I've known her.
She is a walking miracle of God's grace and mercy
and a living example of one who has lived unselfishly for others.

CONTENTS

01
INTRODUCTION TO PAUL'S LETTER TO THE PHILIPPIANS

Personal stories are the stuff of life. Think about it. Generally speaking, are you more engaged when a professor talks about a theory or when he recounts a funny experience from fourth grade? It's one thing to read a few facts about a person's life in the obituaries. It's another to read a biography of why his life mattered. The letter to the Philippians is a compelling book, in part because Paul provides several autobiographical glimpses into his own life. And he uses these personal reflections as well as the examples of others to depict what joy-filled, gospel-focused spiritual maturity looks like.

THE AUTHOR: WHAT WERE PAUL'S CIRCUMSTANCES?

First, in order to understand this book, we should consider Paul's own situation. The apostle wrote this letter from prison, several times mentioning his "bonds" (Phil. 1:7, 13, 14, 16). His captivity was well-known to Roman officials, as he indicates with the phrase "manifest in all the palace" (1:13). In addition, there were professing believers who opposed Paul and were trying to make his condition worse (1:16). They harbored "envy and strife" against him (1:15).

Though confined and opposed in ways that would discourage most, Paul was optimistic. He rejoiced that Christ was being proclaimed, even if some of the evangelists' underlying motivation was antagonistic toward him (1:16–18). Furthermore, he believed that "through [the Philippians'] prayer, and the supply of the Spirit of Jesus Christ," he would be delivered (1:19). (The word *salvation* does not refer to deliverance of his soul from sin but deliverance of his body from prison.) Paul acknowledged that God might choose to honor Himself through Paul's death (1:20), and the prospect of departing and being with Christ appealed to him (1:23). He declared, "To die is gain" (1:21). But the apostle was persuaded that God still had ministry for him to do "for [the Philippians'] furtherance and joy of faith" (1:25). Therefore, throughout this letter Paul conveys a hopeful expectation of release and further service for the Lord. Its outlook differs from 2 Timothy, in which Paul declares that his death is imminent (2 Tim. 4:6).

Why is Paul's personal situation significant for understanding what he says in his letter? How can we relate even if we are not in prison for our faith?

_____

_____

_____

_____

_____

—personal question   —group question

THE RECIPIENTS: WHAT WAS THE PHILIPPIANS' STORY?

Paul was not writing to strangers but to a church God had used him to start. The circumstances surrounding the emergence of this local church and the ongoing relationship they maintained with Paul provide additional context for understanding what Paul says to the recipients of this letter. Their spiritual story consists of a divinely-ordained mission field, divinely-empowered evangelism, and an ongoing ministry partnership.

A Divinely-Ordained Mission Field

Paul and his co-laborers were traveling through Asia Minor (today Turkey) when God the Spirit prevented them from continuing (Acts 16:7). So the missionary team, which included at least Silas and Timothy, took an alternate route to Troas, where Paul experienced what we know as "the Macedonian vision" (16:9). This series of divinely authored events convinced the missionaries—whom the author Luke has now joined, as indicated by the "we" in 16:10—that "the Lord had called [them] to preach the gospel unto [the Macedonians]" (16:10). For the first time in recorded history, the good news of Jesus Christ was entering Europe.

In a matter of days, Paul and his coworkers arrived in Philippi, "the chief city of that part of Macedonia, and a colony" (16:12). Philippi's status as a Roman colony was a big deal. Its people enjoyed the rights of Roman citizenship, such as property ownership. Paul alludes to this status in his letter with the word *conversation*, which means *citizenship* (Phil. 1:27; 3:20). However, although Philippi was fairly strong politically, it was weak religiously. As was his custom, on his first Sabbath in town Paul attempted to minister "to the Jew first" (Rom. 1:16). But there was no synagogue for them to visit, meaning there were in Philippi fewer than the ten male Jews necessary to constitute a synagogue (Acts 16:13).

*Discuss the significance of God's directing
Paul's missionary travels into Europe.*

_____

_____

_____

_____

_____

*Was it appropriate for Paul to begin his
evangelism with the Jews? If so, why?*

_____

_____

_____

_____

Divinely-Empowered Evangelism

In spite of this lack of Jewish influence, God was at work. A businesswoman from Thyatira named Lydia "worshipped God" and heard Paul's company speaking to devout women at a place of prayer "by a river side" (Acts 16:13–14). The Lord "opened" her heart to believe, and "she was baptized, and her household" (16:15). Meanwhile, Paul exorcised a demonic spirit out of a slave girl who "brought her masters much gain" by telling fortunes (16:16–18). These owners subsequently captured and dragged Paul and Silas to the city magistrates to be punished for upending local religious customs. A mob joined the fray, and the officials ruled that the missionaries should be beaten and imprisoned (16:19–24).

It was in that Philippian jail that one of the most famous events in the apostle's entire ministry occurred. Instead of seething in anger or sulking in pity, Paul and his colleague Silas prayed and sang to God. Their faith was accompanied by an earthquake that broke the prisoners free from their shackles. But when the jailer thought all was lost, Paul rushed to assure him that no prisoner had fled. This series of providences prompted the jailer to ask, "Sirs, what must I do to be saved?" (16:25–30). The jailer took his Christian prisoners home, and he and his entire household believed on the Lord Jesus Christ and were baptized (16:31–34). The following day the magistrates released Paul and then with embarrassment ushered him out of town after learning he was actually a Roman citizen just like them (16:35–40).

What lessons should we learn from how God empowered Paul's evangelism in Philippi?

_____

_____

_____

_____

Ongoing Ministry Partnership

The Philippian church that began in Lydia's home maintained a close relationship with Paul. His close connection with these believers is also evident by the multiple visits he made on his way to and from Greece (Acts 20:1–6). Perhaps more than any other church, they supported Paul financially (2 Cor. 11:9), even after he left the Macedonian region (Phil. 4:15). This church also supported the apostle repeatedly when he was ministering in nearby Thessalonica (4:16), instead of assuming that was the Thessalonians' responsibility.

This combination of spiritual and physical help prompted Paul to thank God every time he remembered the Philippians because of their "fellowship in the gospel from the first day until now" (Phil. 1:5). Their interest in the advance of the gospel is as evident as any local church mentioned in the New Testament. And this tangible, heartfelt support is the primary circumstance that prompted Paul to write his epistle.

Because of their concern for Paul's well-being as a prisoner in Rome, the Philippian believers sent Epaphroditus eight hundred miles as a messenger to care for Paul's needs (2:25). By this act of love the Philippians displayed once again their concern for Paul, and this sacrificial effort gave Paul reason to "[rejoice] in the Lord greatly" (4:10). He commends them for sharing in the affliction he was enduring (4:14) and considers his situation to "abound" in light of their gift (4:18). They had done more than could be expected to express thanks for God's grace and provide assistance for the spread of Christ's gospel.

What does Scripture teach us through the example of the Philippians about what it means to have "fellowship in the gospel" (Phil. 1:5)? What could your group do to embrace this kind of participation?

THE PURPOSE: WHY DID PAUL WRITE THIS LETTER?

A Letter of Gratitude

Paul wrote the Philippians with several goals in mind. First, as mentioned earlier, he wanted to thank them for their gift of love. He tells them of his prayers of thanksgiving for them (1:4). Their gift not only ministered to a missionary's needs but brought pleasure to God, like some of the fragrant sacrifices of the Old Covenant (4:18). Their gift was an act of worship. Furthermore, Paul assures them, "My God shall supply all your need according to his riches in glory by Christ Jesus" (4:19). The apostle could not reimburse them for their kindness, but the God who blessed him through their sacrificial gift would bless them too.

> *In his epistles Paul often mentions not only the fact that he has prayed for his recipients but also the content of what he prays. (For example, see Ephesians 1:15–23 or Colossians 1:9–14). How could you apply Paul's practice this week?*

_____

_____

_____

_____

A Letter of Assurance

In addition to expressing his gratitude, Paul wanted to assure the Philippians of God's merciful control of his circumstances and theirs. Though Paul's situation was difficult, God was using his imprisonment and the adversity of other professing believers to spread the gospel (1:12–18). Epaphroditus had nearly died in bringing the Philippians' gift to Paul in Rome, but God spared this faithful messenger's life and spared the apostle from great sorrow by healing him. Therefore, Paul sent Epaphroditus back with his letter to the Philippians so that they could stop worrying and rejoice too (2:25–30). Paul also reassures his readers that he is content in whatever circumstances God places him and that he is taken care of (4:11–13, 18). Through this letter Paul intends to persuade the Philippians to transition from anxiety to trust. In words that have become familiar, he says, "Be careful [anxious] for nothing" (4:6).

> *Read Philippians 4:6–7. What is the antidote to worry? Besides petitions (requests), what should our prayers include? How can you apply this personally?*

A Letter of Exhortation

A third aspect of his purpose is to exhort readers to be unified in the faith. Evidently, there was some divisiveness among the Philippian believers and the potential for more, because unity is a significant theme. He even mentions two women, Euodias and Syntyche, who needed to "be of the same mind in the Lord" (4:2). We do not know the nature of their disagreement, but it was significant enough for Paul to mention them specifically.

A Letter of Warning

This unity for the sake of the gospel was important, in part, because the churches are vulnerable to false teaching. Therefore, a fourth goal is to expose theological error and charge believers to be wary of it. The false teachers apparently were emphasizing the necessity of circumcision (3:2–3). Consequently, Paul responds to this Judaizing error by using his personal testimony to explain justification by faith in Christ alone (3:4–9) and to urge the Philippians to persevere in the true gospel (3:10–16). These "enemies of the cross of Christ" were focused on earthly pursuits, but a believer's most important citizenship is in heaven (3:18–21).

> WOVEN THROUGHOUT THE LETTER ARE THE TWIN STRANDS OF MAINTAINING A GOSPEL FOCUS AND EXPERIENCING CHRISTIAN JOY.

CONCLUSION

Woven throughout the letter are the twin strands of maintaining a gospel focus and experiencing Christian joy. The book of Philippians teaches us to *think* Christianly and confirms that by living this way we experience true *joy*. As one commentary puts it, "Christian joy comes through having a Christ-centered mind."[1] In this letter Paul motivates through autobiography. Each chapter includes passages where Paul speaks reflectively about his own spiritual experience. He also puts forward other faithful examples, like Timothy and Epaphroditus (2:19–30). The tie that binds together these goals and literary features is

---

[1] Roger Ellsworth, *Opening Up Philippians* (Leominster, UK: Day One Publications, 2004), 13.

Paul's overarching purpose of showing what joy-filled, gospel-focused spiritual maturity looks like. What does it take to live in a way that promotes the gospel, trusts God instead of worrying, demonstrates unity with other believers, and avoids destructive theological error? Paul tells us in Philippians.

*Have various members of your group look up these references that mention **joy** or **rejoicing**: Philippians 1:4, 18, 25; 2:2, 17–18, 28–29; 3:1; 4:1, 4. What do these verses teach us about the source and circumstances of joy?*

RECOMMENDED READING

In preparation for the next study chapter, read the entire passage, Philippians 1:27–2:18. Write down any ways in which these verses connect to the major themes discussed above.

NOTES

02
LIVE WORTHY OF THE GOSPEL

PHILIPPIANS 1:27–30

Only let your conversation be as it becometh the gospel of Christ: that whether I come and see you, or else be absent, I may hear of your affairs, that ye stand fast in one spirit, with one mind striving together for the faith of the gospel; and in nothing terrified by your adversaries: which is to them an evident token of perdition, but to you of salvation, and that of God. For unto you it is given in the behalf of Christ, not only to believe on him, but also to suffer for his sake; having the same conflict which ye saw in me, and now hear to be in me.

After expressing his passionate prayer for their spiritual maturity (Phil. 1:3–11) and describing the advance of the gospel through his imprisonment under Roman guard (1:12–26), Paul addresses the Philippians. What can *they* do to participate in the advance of the gospel? He earnestly commands the Philippian believers to live worthy of the gospel of Christ. We are responsible to obey that same command.

WHAT IS PAUL'S CHARGE?

PHILIPPIANS 1:27

Only let your conversation be as it becometh the gospel of Christ.

WORD STUDY

let your conversation be—to live out one's citizenship

becometh—worthily; fittingly; suitably

The phrase translated "let your conversation be" sounds like an exhortation concerning our speech. But *conversation* actually refers to our *how we live as citizens*. At the heart of this term is the Greek word for city, *polis*. Paul appeals to his readers' sense of citizenship because they were a privileged people. Unlike many in the Roman world, the Philippians enjoyed the distinction of Roman citizenship thanks to the conquest and colonization of Octavian (who later became Caesar Augustus). Their status in the Roman Empire entailed significant benefits, and they would have understood that with privilege comes responsibility.

So Paul draws on their sense of civic duty to exhort them to live in a manner worthy of the gospel. His premise is that believers are not only members of a political nation on earth. We are citizens of heaven (Phil. 3:20). He charges us to exercise our heavenly citizenship by properly reflecting what children of God are like and how they should live. We believe the gospel is our identity, so we must live like it. And this gospel living is so important to Paul that he begins Philippians 1:27 with the word *only*. He has much to say in his letter to the Philippians, but his central focus is that we participate in the advance of Christ's gospel by living in a way that corresponds to our faith.

What are some of the duties of a citizen of heaven? How does this metaphor help us understand what it means to be a Christian?

_____

_____

_____

_____

_____

Paul directs us to live in a manner that is worthy of the gospel. Yet we know ourselves to be sinners. Paul himself said, "In me (that is, in my flesh,) dwelleth no good thing" (Rom. 7:18). Therefore, what does Paul's command in Philippians 1:27 not mean? If we are not worthy in ourselves, how can we live worthy of the gospel?

_____

_____

_____

_____

_____

HOW DO WE LIVE THIS WAY?

PHILIPPIANS 1:27

. . . that whether I come and see you, or else be absent, I may hear of your affairs, that ye stand fast in one spirit, with one mind striving together for the faith of the gospel.

WORD STUDY

stand fast—to stand firm; to persevere; to persist

spirit—not the Holy Spirit but a man's inner spirit; the soul

mind—soul

with one mind—the group is united in heart about a matter

striving together—to work together (side by side); to contend together; to labor with

Paul's singular, consuming passion was to hear that the Philippians were living worthy of the gospel whether or not he saw them again. He hoped to visit the Philippian church after his release from prison, but he knew the Roman government might execute him first. Either way, he wanted to hear that they were faithful, effective witnesses for Christ in their community. What directions does Paul give? What does faithful gospel living require?

First, the passage indicates that living worthy of the gospel means taking *a courageous stance*. We have to "stand fast in one spirit" (1:27). The *spirit* could refer to the Holy Spirit but probably means a person's inner being. Deep within each believer must be a commitment to pursue God's purposes alongside other believers. Paul encourages us to be "in nothing terrified by [our] adversaries" (1:28). We cannot expect to live as citizens of heaven without encountering hostility from hell. That would be like living in Israel and assuming undisturbed peace with the Middle East. At the same time, we do not need to be fearful. We must simply trust God and take courage that "greater is he that is in [us], than he that is in the world" (1 John 4:4).

> *What contemporary challenges to the gospel can tempt us to be fearful? Why is it important that we stand firm?*

_____

_____

_____

_____

Second, living worthy of the gospel means maintaining *a united mindset*. Participating in the advance of the gospel requires a unified, cooperative effort of the entire congregations in personal and corporate evangelism. The gospel cannot be believed if it is not first proclaimed (Rom. 10:13–15). The duty of the church is clear: if it doesn't evangelize, it will inevitably fossilize! Those who spread the good news, however, must overcome the greatest barrier—paralyzing fear of rejection. Those who oppose the gospel often intimidate the witnesses of Christ, resulting in the potential shutdown of evangelism.

THE DUTY OF THE CHURCH IS CLEAR: IF IT DOESN'T EVANGELIZE, IT WILL INEVITABLY FOSSILIZE!

Remaining united about "the faith of the gospel" is utterly crucial. An army that can sever the enemy forces in two has a much better chance of victory. A herd of gazelle in an African savannah are strong when together but vulnerable when separated. Christian unity in the gospel is important for many reasons, not the least of which is the advance of the gospel itself. "The faith" is core Christian belief centered on the gospel. It has been handed down from one generation to the next for two thousand years. Ensuring its continued advance hinges on a united, unwavering mindset. Good news that is not proclaimed ceases to be news. It's still true. It's still amazing. But no one hears about it.

Look up 2 Timothy 1:12–14 and 2:1–2. Write down the succession of people who treasured the gospel and then entrusted it to someone else. Are you intentionally seeking ways to proclaim the good news of Jesus Christ? Is there someone to whom you should be entrusting the gospel?

_____

_____

_____

List three reasons you are afraid to share the gospel.

_____

_____

_____

_____

WHAT MOTIVATES THIS GOSPEL-CENTERED LIVING?

PHILIPPIANS 1:28–30

And in nothing terrified by your adversaries: which is to them an evident token of perdition, but to you of salvation, and that of God. For unto you it is given in the behalf of Christ, not only to believe on him, but also to suffer for his sake; having the same conflict which ye saw in me, and now hear to be in me.

WORD STUDY

terrified—to be frightened or intimidated; sometimes used in regard to spooking horses; may carry the idea of "throwing into consternation"

an evident token—sign (as in *omen*); proof

perdition—destruction; waste; ruin; carries the idea of the utter ruin of those who do not believe

given—graciously granted; bestowed

suffer—to experience discomfort from an outside source; to be affected; to feel

conflict—struggle; fight; battle; athletic metaphor referring to contesting for the gospel

JUST AS FAITH IS A DIVINE GIFT, FREELY GIVEN BY A SOVEREIGN GOD, SO SUFFERING IS A DIVINE GIFT FROM THE LORD.

Paul gives two compelling reasons for us to be courageous and united in the face of our adversaries. First, opposition to the gospel is a sure sign that the messengers are truly God's people. "Blessed are they which are persecuted for righteousness' sake: for theirs is the kingdom of heaven" (Matt. 5:10). Christians must take a courageous stance for the gospel, but persecution is inevitable for all who choose to live godly in Christ Jesus (2 Tim. 3:12). While the destruction of God's enemies is sure, our salvation is equally as secure (Phil. 1:28). Those who oppose the gospel are proving that they are under conviction because of their sins. As they fight God's work, their consciences cry out against them, making them aware that they are under divine judgment. Paul remembered the conviction he experienced prior to his conversion when he persecuted the church and stoned Stephen (Acts 7:58). Prior to his conversion, the Philippian jailer must also have experienced deep conviction because of his participation in the beating and imprisonment of Paul and Silas (Acts 16:23). God works in the hearts of those who fight against Him; therefore, believers never need to be intimidated.

Second, persecution introduces believers to a new spiritual dimension of grace. Paul compared the grace of suffering to the grace of salvation. Just as faith is a divine gift, freely given by a sovereign God, so suffering is a divine gift from the Lord. The Philippians faced the same heroic struggle of standing for the gospel in spite of persecution that Paul and Jesus had experienced. Those who stand for the gospel experience "the fellowship of his sufferings" (Phil. 3:10). The Philippian believers were counted worthy to suffer with the apostle and with their Lord. We should never be intimidated by the world's opposition to the gospel, because "great is [our] reward in heaven" (Matt. 5:12). The gospel by which Christ rescued us from death is a gospel worth living for courageously and unitedly.

CONCLUSION

What are some everyday ways that your life can be "worthy of the gospel of Christ"?

_____

_____

_____

_____

_____

According to Philippians 1:29, what two gifts has God granted? What point is he trying to emphasize by associating the two gifts?

_____

_____

_____

_____

_____

RECOMMENDED READING

In preparation for the next chapter, read Ephesians 4:1–6. List the characteristics of "walk[ing] worthy of the vocation wherewith ye are called" (4:1).

_____
_____
_____
_____
_____

List the truths in verses 4–6 that unite God's people.

_____
_____
_____
_____

NOTES

03
BE LIKE-MINDED

PHILIPPIANS 2:1−2
*If there be therefore any consolation in Christ, if any comfort of love,
if any fellowship of the Spirit, if any bowels and mercies, fulfill ye my
joy, that ye be likeminded, having the same love, being of one accord,
of one mind.*

One of the most famous trio of leaders in history was the First Triumvirate of Roman politicians Pompey, Crassus, and Julius Caesar. Although they formed an alliance, each had personal ambition, not joint success, supremely in mind. For a few years in the 50s BC they combined forces, but their political cohesion unraveled into outright rivalry and civil war. Eventually Caesar crossed the Rubicon and defeated Pompey at Pharsalus. These men were similar in their aspirations for glory, but history bears the evidence that they did not share a unified mindset. Allies became enemies.

Disunity has destroyed countless teams, companies, churches, and homes. Perhaps you are familiar with a church that has suffered severely from selfish division. The sign in front of the church building professed the gospel, but the relationships inside failed to apply it. Very few things hinder the advance of the gospel as much as a disunified church or home.

Paul said the first aspect of living worthy of the gospel was the Philippians' *external relationship* to the world by their standing

fast and cooperating together to advance the gospel in the face
of opposition (1:27–30). He goes on in the first two verses of
Philippians 2 to address the second aspect of living worthy of
the gospel—an *internal unity* within the body of the church,
and he commands them to be like-minded. With this exhortation Paul more fully explains what he meant by contending for
the gospel "in one spirit, with one mind" (1:27). In order to
live in a manner worthy of the gospel, we have to pursue unity
with fellow believers.

SPIRITUAL UNITY IS THE BYPRODUCT OF BELIEVERS WITHIN THE CHURCH BODY WHO LOVE EACH OTHER.

This call to unity was
directly applicable to
the Philippian church.
When Epaphroditus told
him about the condition
of the Philippian church,
Paul became deeply con-
cerned about the brew-
ing conflict between
two ladies, Euodias and
Syntyche, two of his co-laborers in the ministry (4:2). By
this exhortation to unity Paul responds to the disruption and
potential division in the church because of the unresolved
conflict.

THE REASONS FOR UNITY

PHILIPPIANS 2:1–2
*If there be therefore any consolation in Christ, if any
comfort of love, if any fellowship of the Spirit, if any
bowels and mercies, fulfill ye my joy.*

WORD STUDY

consolation—comfort; encouragement; solace

comfort—consolation

fellowship—close relationship; participation; communion

bowels—inward affection; kindness; sympathy

mercies—pity; compassion; longings; manifestations of pity

Christian unity is impossible without spiritual motivation and divine enablement. Therefore, Paul not only commands the Philippian believers to be like-minded but also provides several reasons. First of all, Paul bases his appeal on a theological premise—the unity among the Father, the Son, and the Holy Spirit. Paul mentions both Christ and the Spirit explicitly, and God the Father is implicit in the reference to "any comfort of love" (2:1). Although three distinct persons comprise the Trinity, there is only one God. These three persons experience a perfect unity.

Secondly, during their sufferings in Philippi, the believers shared the same spiritual blessings that flowed from their common relationship with the Trinity. The first phrase, "consolation in Christ," refers to the comfort and encouragement we have as saints "in Christ Jesus" (1:1). The second phrase, "comfort of love," speaks of God's consoling love for His people who often face pressure, as did the Philippians. The third phrase, "fellowship of the Spirit," signifies that the Holy Spirit indwells us and brings us into communion with the triune God. The final phrase, "bowels and mercies," depicts God's undeserved and tender compassion for the church, like a mother for her newborn baby.

The word *any* precedes each of these phrases. In other words, Paul grounds his appeal for unity in the spiritual blessings the Philippians knew to be true. If the persons of the Trinity are unified and work together for the benefit of God's suffering children, shouldn't those children possess and express the same unity in their relationships with each other in the body of the church?

Describe the significance of the following terms
for being like-minded.

consolation

_____

comfort

_____

fellowship

_____

bowels

_____

mercies

_____

What role does Philippians 2:1 play in Paul's
reasoning? What makes his argument effective?

_____

_____

_____

_____

Thirdly, Paul commands like-mindedness for the completion
of his own joy. Does his command sound selfish? It shouldn't
when we understand God's overarching intent in this letter
to the Philippians. For all believers of all time, God put Paul
on display as _the Christlike model of joyful Christian matu-
rity._ Paul is our paradigm—our standard of joy. (The word _joy_

appears sixteen times in this epistle.) True joy is not the result of easy circumstances, so Paul rejoiced in a variety of contexts (4:10–13). Joy is focused on God's glory, so Paul's joy could not be complete if the church whom he dearly loved was not thriving in gospel unity for Christ's sake.

> *What usually brings you joy? What could you give greater attention to in order to align your joy with God's glory?*

_____

_____

_____

_____

THE ESSENCE OF UNITY

PHILIPPIANS 2:2

. . . that ye be likeminded, having the same love, being of one accord, of one mind.

WORD STUDY

like-minded—to think; to ponder; to be of the same mind to feel

love—charity; benevolence; brotherly love

one accord—united in spirit; harmonious

Paul reveals that true joy is found in the Lord (4:4) and in His work in the world. One way the Lord cultivates joy among believers is through the unity of Christian brotherhood. Paul declares that his spiritual cup of joy will overflow if the Philippian believers are like-minded. "Behold, how good and how pleasant it is for brethren to dwell together in unity!" (Ps. 133:1). The essence of unity is like-mindedness.

What exactly is *like-mindedness*? Clearly, it is not agreement of opinion on all facets of life. In another context Paul speaks positively of both Christians who eat for God's glory and Christians who abstain from eating for God's glory (Rom. 14:5–6). When a church today is renovating its auditorium, it is okay to differ on whether the new carpet should be gray or beige as long as God is the one they are most concerned about! Nor does like-mindedness describe a group of believers who all look alike, dress alike, or talk alike. That state is called *uniformity*. Rather, like-mindedness has to do with the dispositions that foster unity and the decisions we make because of these attitudes.

> *Throughout his letter to the Philippians, Paul emphasizes the importance of how we think. We have already considered the gospel mindset Paul urges in Philippians 1:27. Look up these additional references and summarize what they teach us about a Christian mindset. Then pick one passage to meditate on and discuss with your group.*

Philippians 2:5–8—thinking and Christ

_____

_____

_____

_____

_____

Philippians 3:12–15—thinking and mature believers

_____

_____

_____

_____

_____

Philippians 3:17–21—thinking and earthly desires

_____

_____

_____

_____

Philippians 4:6–7—thinking and prayer

_____

_____

_____

_____

Philippians 4:8—thinking and its characteristics

_____

_____

_____

_____

_____

Philippians 4:10–13—thinking and contentment

_____

_____

_____

_____

_____

Paul describes this unity with four phrases in Philippians 2:2—"[1] be likeminded, [2] having the same love, [3] being of one accord, [4] of one mind." The first and fourth phrases use similar wording with a slight variation: the first phrase means "to think the same;" the fourth means "to think the one." Combining these ideas, we are "to like-mindedly mind the one thing." The phrase "being of one accord" means "to be of the same soul," referring to the inner man. These phrases, however, do not fully capture Paul's meaning.

The key to understanding like-mindedness is found in the phrase "having the same love." That phrase doesn't mean that all Christians should like the same things. Whether you prefer Mac or PC or neither is irrelevant when

SPIRITUAL UNITY IS THE BYPRODUCT OF BELIEVERS WITHIN THE CHURCH BODY WHO LOVE EACH OTHER.

it comes to Christian unity. Rather, we should have the same love for one another. Unity is possible—and necessary—regardless of our differences in age or ethnicity or background. We manifest this attitude of unity when we love one another with a selfless, sacrificial love. "And above all these things put on charity [love], which is the bond of perfectness" (Col. 3:14).

Love is the glue that holds God's people together, and spiritual unity is the byproduct of believers within the church body who love each other.

It is of utmost importance that we participate in the advance of the gospel by living worthy of our heavenly citizenship. This manner of life requires unity found in like-mindedness. And this mindset is possible because we are fellow participants in God's gracious salvation. Our Father has promised to finish the good work He has begun in us (Phil. 1:6)—a corporate building project that brings diverse sinners into loving unity with God and one another for the sake of the gospel.

What is the fundamental thing on which Christians should be unified? Explain how it unifies believers? What are some particular challenges you face in terms of Christian unity?

_____

_____

_____

_____

_____

Is it possible to be "of one mind" and yet disagree on some things? What truth(s) from Philippians 2:1–2 could you help you in this situation?

_____

_____

_____

_____

_____

RECOMMENDED READING

In preparation for the next chapter, read James 4:6–10. List the actions of a humble person.

_____

_____

_____

_____

_____

NOTES

04
THE CALL TO HUMILITY

PHILIPPIANS 2:3–4

Let nothing be done through strife or vainglory; but in lowliness of mind let each esteem other better than themselves. Look not every man on his own things, but every man also on the things of others.

Jesus and His disciples were making their way to Jerusalem. In anticipation of Christ's coronation, James and John decided it was time to angle for the most prestigious positions they could imagine—sitting on either side of Jesus in the kingdom (Mark 10:37). Matthew records that their mother even knelt down to petition Christ for these honors (Matt. 20:20–21). She wanted her sons to have the best spots too. Jesus told them they didn't realize what they were asking (Mark 10:38). He could promise them a *baptism*, by which He meant death for proclaiming the Truth, but their rank in glory was not His to give.

The situation angered the other disciples (Mark 10:41). The aspiration and audacity of the so-called Sons of Thunder ran roughshod over the other disciples' own self-focused agendas. They had all laid aside other pursuits to follow Christ and wanted recognition for doing so.

Then Jesus called them together to readjust their thinking. In earthly kingdoms the "great ones exercise authority" (Mark

10:42). Importance is measured in terms of power. But it's different in God's kingdom. Success means ministry. It means subordinating yourself, not just to the Master but also to your fellow servants. Jesus said, "Whosoever of you will be the chiefest, shall be servant of all" (Mark 10:44).

HUMILITY IS THE ESSENCE OF A CHRISTLIKE DISPOSITION.

What was true for Jesus' original disciples is no less true for the rest of the church Christ bought with His blood. In Philippians 2 Paul presses forward with his appeal for living worthy of the gospel by exhorting his readers to interact humbly with one another. A unified mindset requires humility, because humility is the essence of a Christlike disposition. The *like-mindedness* Paul commands all believers to have is a *low-mindedness*. Paul describes this gospel-focused humility in Philippians 2:3–4 and illustrates it in verses 5–11 with the example of Jesus Christ.

WHAT HUMILITY IS NOT

PHILIPPIANS 2:3
Let nothing be done through strife or vainglory.

WORD STUDY

strife—selfish ambition; selfish rivalry; aspiration without consideration or care for others

vainglory—vanity; self-conceit; excessive ambition

In order to understand what humility is, we must be clear on what it is not. First of all, humility is not a self-deprecating attitude that means we have a low view of ourselves. In fact, thinking about ourselves isn't part of a humble attitude at all. Secondly, Paul declares that a lowly mind is never motivated by "strife or vainglory." A good illustration of strife is a politician who runs for office, ambitiously courts popular opinion, and competitively positions himself to win the race against any rival. He cares only about himself and is driven by selfish ambition. In fact, he resents the success of others and works to demonstrate his superiority.

Paul had experienced this kind of opposition personally. While he was in prison some fellow believers attempted to antagonize him by proclaiming Christ (Phil. 1:16–17). They evidently were jealous of Paul and territorial about their sphere of ministry. Perhaps they judged him inferior because he had landed in prison, and they wanted to highlight this supposed weakness. Even though Paul designated this attitude as a work of the flesh (Gal. 5:20), he rejoiced that the gospel was being proclaimed, regardless of their motivation (Phil. 1:18). Yet, even though he was commendably gracious in his response to these rivals in Rome, Paul insisted that the Philippians recognize how damaging such a mentality is to Christian unity. Unity cannot coexist with this kind of ambition.

Look up James 3:14–16 and list the similarities and differences between Paul's exhortation and James's.

_____

_____

_____

_____

_____

How easy is it to view the accomplishment of a fellow believer and be tempted to cut him down to size so that you don't feel inferior? Are you tempted in this area? Do you need to ask for forgiveness from someone you are treating this way?

_____

_____

_____

_____

_____

Similarly, a vainglorious person is motivated by selfish conceit. He has an inflated opinion of himself and lives only for the empty opinions and praise of others. After the Pharisees gave their money to God, a trumpet was blown in the temple in order to announce their contribution. Jesus declared, "They have their reward" (Matt. 6:2). Again, this kind of pride is the manifestation of our flesh (Gal. 5:26). If we do not want to be proud, we must "walk in the spirit" (Gal. 5:25). Humble people are never motivated by self-interest because their minds are set on the advancement of the gospel, not on the advancement of their personal agendas. Paul forbids these forms of pride in the strongest of terms by using an emphatic double negative in Greek. We could translate the phrase as if a father were communicating a sober warning to his child: "Never ever act this way."

Explain the terms strife *and* vainglory.
Contrast these to lowliness of mind *(Phil. 2:3).*

_____

_____

_____

_____

_____

WHAT HUMILITY IS

PHILIPPIANS 2:3–4

. . . but in lowliness of mind let each esteem other better than themselves. Look not every man on his own things, but every man also on the things of others.

WORD STUDY

lowliness of mind—humility; modesty

esteem—to think; to consider

better—to have power over; to surpass; to excel

look—to look out for; to keep one's eyes on; to consider

We can often detect pride, especially in other people. A basketball player brags about how many points he scored. A musician smugly assumes her position as first chair. A politician runs a smear campaign against his opponent. A student laughs about how easy a certain class is. But what is humility? Is it simply avoiding "strife and vainglory"? As Paul continues his exhortation, he alludes to three positive elements of humility.

First, Paul describes humility in terms of *what we value.* The antidote to selfishness and pride is placing the importance of others ahead of our own. Paul is not suggesting that we grow careless about our own physical or spiritual well-being. It is virtually impossible, not to mention hazardous, not to have any concern for yourself. But we need to prioritize our values by ranking others ahead of ourselves. In other words, when humility is our attitude, we will regard our fellow brothers and sisters in Christ as the standouts, not ourselves. We will sincerely celebrate the success of others instead of maneuvering so that they notice our own. We will praise God for what He is doing through others and not take credit for what He may be doing through us. We will honor the legitimate preferences of others instead of insisting that everyone is aware of our own. This is what Paul means by his phrase in Romans 12:10, "in honour preferring one another."

Read Romans 12:9–21 and list the ways we can humbly show love to others.

_____

_____

_____

_____

_____

How can you practically "esteem other[s] better" than yourself? (Phil. 2:3) How does someone who has a lowly mind act at home, at work, or at college? What is the relationship between humility and personal success?

_____

_____

_____

Next Paul describes humility in terms of *what concerns us*. He states, "Look not every man on his own things, but every man also on the things of others" (Phil. 2:4). As stated above, humility does not mean talking about yourself in a derogatory way. Humility means not focusing on yourself to begin with. To "look . . . on the things of others" is to give careful attention to their needs. For example, when a man notices that a woman is walking behind him entering a building, he anticipates an opportunity to show consideration and holds open the door.

He puts his own desires not to waste time and not to put in more effort than the next guy in their proper place, because he is looking out for the interests of others, not just his own.

Paul recognizes that each of us has to give some attention to his own needs. (Note the word *also* in verse 4.) And he acknowledges that very few believers consistently display this mindset, as he mentions when commending Timothy (Phil. 2:21). But neither of these realities impedes Paul from directing us to get our eyes off ourselves so that we can "bear . . . one another's burdens, and so fulfil the law of Christ" (Gal. 6:2). This kind of *one-another* ministry is essential to unity.

> *List one interest of each person in your group. Describe how you can* look on *those interests while laying your own interests aside.*

_____

_____

_____

_____

Ultimately, Paul describes humility in terms of *how we view ourselves.* Humility is "lowliness of mind." It is when we lay ourselves low, like a doormat, that we are in the best position to receive God's grace (James 4:6). It is also when we bear a striking resemblance to Jesus Christ, who is "meek and *lowly* in heart" (Matt. 11:29).

We find humility best illustrated in the

WE FIND HUMILITY BEST ILLUSTRATED IN THE ATTITUDE OF A SERVANT WHO IS OTHERS-ORIENTED.

attitude of a servant who is others-oriented. The word *lowliness* describes a slave in biblical times. A slave stood on the lowest rung of the social ladder. Everyone else was above a slave. A slave had nothing to do in life but to serve those who were above him. Paul commands Christians to go low and to adopt a slave mentality. He and other New Testament writers showed the way by describing themselves as "a servant [i.e., bondslave] of Jesus Christ" (Rom. 1:1; James 1:1; Jude 1:1).

Those who are truly loving keep the value and importance of other people in the forefront of their minds. Our neighbors are worthy of our sacrificial service to them. We naturally look after our own interests; but when we are humble, we view the needs of others as if they were our own. The primary quality of humility is the way we think about others. *Low-mindedness* is the attitude that enables gospel-centered unity. As Jesus taught James and John and their colleagues, humble service is the counterintuitive path to success for citizens of His heavenly kingdom.

Jesus said, "Learn of me" (Matt. 11:29). In what ways did Christ display a lowly mind?

One way to cultivate low-mindedness is by associating with those whose earthly status is lowly. Do you reach out to those who are less privileged or less socially adept or less academically astute? What is one step you could take this week to humbly build relationships with the humble?

_____

_____

_____

_____

_____

RECOMMENDED READING

In preparation for the next chapter, read and meditate on Philippians 2:5–8. Discuss at least one truth from the passage in anticipation of the next chapter.

_____

_____

_____

_____

_____

NOTES

05
THINKING LIKE CHRIST

PHILIPPIANS 2:5–8

*Let this mind be in you, which was also in Christ Jesus: Who, being
in the form of God, thought it not robbery to be equal with God:
but made himself of no reputation, and took upon him the form of
a servant, and was made in the likeness of men: and being found in
fashion as a man, he humbled himself, and became obedient unto
death, even the death of the cross.*

Philippians 2:5–11 is the high point of this section of Paul's letter. In fact, it is one of the grandest and loftiest Christological
passages in the entire Bible. These verses can be compared to an
exquisite piece of jewelry—a beautiful diamond in a 24-carat
gold setting. Many theologians have published rich theological
volumes about this passage. Verses 6–11 follow a simple struc-
ture that dives downward and then soars upward. In verses
6–8 Paul describes the descent of Christ Jesus from the realms
of divine glory to the humiliation of a criminal's cross. In
verses 9–11 Paul explains the ascent of Christ Jesus to an even
more exalted status as the risen Lord. Very few passages in the
New Testament depict the person and work of Christ in such
descriptive, compelling
language.

Yet their renown for rich
theology can obscure
the straightforward
purpose of these verses
in Philippians 2. Paul's

PAUL'S PRIMARY INTENTION . . . WAS TO PRESENT JESUS AS THE EXAMPLE OF A HUMBLE MIND.

primary intention in writing them was to present Jesus as the example of a humble mind. The apostle could have written scores of pages of exhortation and rebuke in response to the Philippians' bickering and anxiety. But instead, he turned their attention to the very essence of the gospel, summed up in a three-word phrase—look to Jesus. Paul does not address our need for humble unity by scathing rebuke or flawless logic. The most powerful argument—the most compelling reason for us to live distinct, transformed lives—is the person and work of Jesus Christ.

Before considering Christ's mindset, we need to understand what Paul means by his imperative, "Let this mind be in you, which was also in Christ Jesus." Does it mean that we automatically think like Jesus because we are united to Him by faith? Or does it mean that Jesus displayed a certain mindset that we must adopt in our relationships with one another? It is true that our union with Christ brings tremendous spiritual benefit. But this particular passage uses parallel language—"in you" and "in Christ"—to emphasize that Christ is our perfect pattern. He is the image to whom we must be conformed (Rom. 8:29). We must think like Him.

> *Put Paul's command in Philippians 2:5 in your own words.*

_____

_____

_____

_____

_____

> *Though similar, there is a difference between trying to imitate someone and being conformed to that person's character. The theme of Christlikeness*

in the New Testament is more like the second than the first. Discuss the difference.

_____

_____

_____

_____

CHRIST HUMBLY GAVE

PHILIPPIANS 2:5–6

Let this mind be in you, which was also in Christ Jesus: Who, being in the form of God, thought it not robbery to be equal with God.

WORD STUDY

let this mind be—to think; to ponder; to set one's mind on

form—outward appearance; shape; "that which truly characterizes a given reality"[1]

thought—to think; to consider

robbery—something to clutch or prize; the act of seizing

equal—same; consistent

So how did Christ think? First of all, Paul provides an insider's glimpse into Jesus' character and mindset prior to His incarnation. Paul states Jesus' deity emphatically: "Who, being in the form of God, thought it not robbery to be equal with God"

---

[1] Gordon Fee, *Paul's Letter to the Philippians*, The New International Commentary on the New Testament (Grand Rapids, MI: Wm. B. Eerdmans Publishing Co., 1995), 204.

(2:6). The phrase "the form of God" refers to Christ's inner character and divine attributes; the essence of His character is the very nature of God. The writer of Hebrews says that the Son of God is "the brightness of *his* [Father's] glory, and the express image of his person" (Heb. 1:3). Paul further confirms this truth by declaring that Christ is perfectly equal with the Father.

So what is the disposition of deity? Even in His eternal state, the Son of God expressed humility in the way He thought. He didn't hold on to His equality with God the Father like one who selfishly clings to a treasure, unwilling to let it go. He didn't hoard things; He gave them away. He "thought it not robbery to be equal with God" (Phil. 2:6). In other words, equality with God does not consist of grasping but of giving away. His disposition is that of a giver.

> *Write out in your own words what Paul meant when he said Jesus "thought it not robbery to be equal with God" (Phil. 2:6). Why is this fact significant?*

> *Look up 2 Corinthians 8:9 and discuss how it reinforces what Philippians 2:6 teaches.*

CHRIST HUMBLY EMPTIED HIMSELF

PHILIPPIANS 2:7

But made himself of no reputation, and took upon him the form of a servant, and was made in the likeness of men.

WORD STUDY

made himself of no reputation—to make empty; to render void

took upon him—to take; to receive

servant—bondslave

likeness—image; form

Paul presents a second aspect of Christ's mindset through His humble incarnation. The humility of God the Son did not remain in glory. Jesus "made himself of no reputation" (2:7). His character, in conjunction with His Father's will, compelled Him to empty Himself—to come to earth and be born as a man. This statement refers to Jesus' surrender of the following privileges and rights in becoming a man:

- the holy atmosphere of heaven

- the display of His eternal glory

- the wealth and privileges of His deity and power

He set all these rights aside to become the Redeemer and Mediator between God and man.

In this self-emptying, Jesus took on the form or essence of a slave. He retained "the form of God" but added to it "the form of a servant." He chose this mindset before His incarnation; and as the promised Messiah, He came as His Father's servant. Seven centuries earlier Isaiah had prophesied the incarnation with these words of God: "Behold my servant, whom I uphold; mine elect, in whom my soul delighteth; I have put my spirit upon him: he shall bring forth judgment to the Gentiles" (Isa. 42:1). While on earth, Jesus confessed, "For I came down from heaven, not to do mine own will, but the will of him that sent me" (John 6:38).

IN ORDER TO UNIFY FOR THE SAKE OF CHRIST'S GOSPEL, CHRIST'S PEOPLE MUST HUMBLY CONFORM TO CHRIST'S MINDSET.

Paul says Jesus "was made in the likeness of men" (Phil. 2:7). The term *likeness* could be misunderstood to convey that Jesus only *appeared* to be human. But Scripture clearly records that Jesus Christ did not merely go through the motions; He fully identified with the human race. He came to earth, "was made a little lower than the angels" (Heb. 2:9), and subjected Himself to all the experiences of weak humanity—hunger, thirst, pain, tears, and death—with one exception. He lacked a sinful nature. Christ exemplified a humble mindset by pouring Himself out for the redemption of sinners.

List some specific instances in the Gospels when Jesus showed how He "made Himself of no reputation" (Phil. 2:7).

_____

_____

_____

_____

CHRIST HUMBLY SUBMITTED HIMSELF

PHILIPPIANS 2:8

*. . . and being found in fashion as a man, he hum-
bled himself, and became obedient unto death, even
the death of the cross.*

WORD STUDY

being found—to find; to discover; He was seen to be

in fashion—outward appearance; form; shape; that which
makes something recognizable; everything in a person
which strikes the senses

he humbled himself—to lower; to make low; to humble;
to humiliate; to take the lowest place

unto—until; as far as; to the point of; to this degree

In verse 8 Paul relates a third aspect of Jesus' humble mindset.
Christ is our example of humility because He is giving, not
grasping. He is our example because He emptied Himself of
deserved privilege. And He is our example because He obeyed
His Father fully. Jesus Christ completed His humble descent
as a man by submitting Himself to the crux of His Father's
will—dying on a cross.

By coming to earth as a man, Jesus Christ unveiled His humility for all the world to see. Had He stooped to become a king,
He still would have been the humblest man who ever lived.
Instead, He took the lowest position in every choice of life. No
one judged Him to be divine by His appearance, and He grew
and developed just like any other child. In His lifestyle, He
chose the path of poverty and suffering. In His ministry, He
reached out to the poor and to society's outcasts. However, we
see the ultimate manifestation of His humility in His complete

obedience to His Father's will when He died on the cross for the sins of the world. He lowered Himself as far as possible when He "became obedient unto death, even the death of the cross" (2:8). To the Roman mind, crucifixion was the vilest death imaginable. A crucified Messiah didn't meet the approval of many Jews either. They assumed Jesus was accursed (Deut. 21:22–23). But that shame paled in comparison with the agony of bearing "the iniquity of us all" and being forsaken by His Father (Isa. 53:6; Matt. 27:46).

Through his account of Christ's descent from heaven to earth to the cross, Paul paints a perfect picture of humility. This kind of attitude unifies the church and fulfills God's command to live worthy the gospel. In order to unify for the sake of Christ's gospel, Christ's people must humbly conform to Christ's mindset.

How can we humble ourselves? According to Christ's example, what are some of the characteristics of a humble person?

What rights or privileges could you forfeit in order to participate in advancing the gospel?

RECOMMENDED READING

The next chapter focuses on the exaltation of Jesus Christ. Read Isaiah 14:12–20 and note the trajectory of the king of Babylon (whom Isaiah seems to liken to Lucifer). How is his attitude different from Christ's? What are the results of his pride?

NOTES

06
GOD EXALTS THE HUMBLE

PHILIPPIANS 2:9–11

Wherefore God also hath highly exalted him, and given him a name which is above every name: that at the name of Jesus every knee should bow, of things in heaven, and things in earth, and things under the earth; and that every tongue should confess that Jesus Christ is Lord, to the glory of God the Father.

One of the most beautiful threads in Scripture's tapestry is how God exalts seemingly insignificant people for His name's sake. Think of Joseph, who was thrown in a pit and sold as a slave and lied and forgotten about before he became the most powerful man in Egypt after Pharaoh. Consider Moses, who went from outlawed baby to a member of Egyptian royalty to outlawed shepherd in the desert to the self-doubting leader of Israel's exodus. Or Ruth, the Moabitess who loyally loved Naomi, preserved the family line, and became an ancestor of the Messiah. Her descendant David fits this pattern too. He was the seventh-born shepherd boy who became Israel's greatest king. Another example is Esther, the attractive Jewish girl in a foreign land who was promoted to queen "for such a time as this" (Esther 4:14).

But the most amazing and important instance of this theme is what Paul describes in Philippians 2. Verses 6–8 reveal the mind of the Son when He emptied and humbled Himself; in verses 9–11, we discover the mind of the Father when He exalted and honored His Son. The Son knew from eternity that

BY THE PERFECT EXAMPLE OF JESUS CHRIST, GOD THE FATHER FOREVER CONFIRMED THE TRUTH THAT HE RAISES UP THE HUMBLE.

He would be the Lamb of God, slain for man's sins. He also knew that He would be exalted to the right hand of the throne of His Father. By the perfect example of Jesus Christ, God the Father forever confirmed the truth that He raises up the humble.

CHRIST'S EXALTED STATUS

PHILIPPIANS 2:9
Wherefore God also hath highly exalted him, and given him a name which is above every name.

WORD STUDY

wherefore—introduces the result of the preceding verses

highly exalted—raised to a high point of honor

given—graciously granted

Christ did not elude or escape death. He met it head-on and conquered it. He charged into the fangs of death and endured the most powerful arsenal the enemy had at his disposal. And His exaltation to the right hand of His Father in glory is clear proof that through His death and resurrection, Christ won the day. As it says in Hebrews 1:3, "When he had by himself purged our sins, sat down on the right hand of the Majesty on high." His victory is complete. It is the greatest triumph of all time.

But in this passage in Philippians 2, Paul emphasizes not only *what* Jesus did but *how* He did it. The Son of God died for our sins on a despicable Roman cross as the suffering Servant. He won, not by pumping Himself up but by pouring Himself out. And that is why God the Father honors the Son in such glorious fashion. The word *wherefore* connects verses 6–8 and 9–11. Christ selflessly chose to lower Himself. As a result, His Father gladly chose to exalt Him.

The Father responded to the Son's redemptive work with two related actions. First, He gave Christ an unparalleled position. He "highly exalted him" (2:9). Because Jesus went to the lowest depths, He was super exalted to the highest position of honor and authority in heaven and in earth. Paul is not teaching that Christ became God again or now possesses more deity than ever before. Remember where Paul's illustration began, with the Son of God in heaven determining to display His equality with God through giving, not grasping (2:6). He laid aside privilege, not deity (2:7). Though this position has always been rightfully His, it was not apparent during the time He humbly ministered in Galilee and died outside Jerusalem. By divine design it was not announced until after He became the God-man, suffered as the propitiation for our sin, and rose from the dead. The Father has ensured that there is no mistake now. He has declared Christ to be in the highest position possible—He is the Lord.

> *Read Acts 2:29–36 to discover when this exaltation took place.*

ᛁᛁ *What does the word* **wherefore** *signify in Paul's logic (Phil. 2:9)?*

_____

_____

_____

_____

Second, when Jesus ascended into heaven, the Father gave Him a title that exceeds all other earthly titles of kings, presidents, prime ministers, and emperors. God honored Christ with the name of *Lord*! No mere human has legitimately aspired to this designation, though some have tried. For example, Alexander the Great accepted the attribution as son of Zeus during a visit to a North African temple. The crazy Roman emperor Caligula also fancied himself as a god. But no person in the history of humanity has been able to elude the sure-fire sign of frail humanity—death. Sin's wages have doomed us all. But Jesus lived a righteous life. He alone conquered death through resurrection. He is in a category by Himself.

What exactly is this name the Father has given the Son? It may initially appear to be His human name, Jesus (Phil. 2:10), but the passage drives toward a different climax. The name of Jesus at which every knee bows is stated emphatically in verse 11: "Jesus Christ is Lord." The Greek word for *Lord* (*kurios*) can simply mean *master*, and Christ is certainly Master of all. But Paul means even more. Drawing from language in Isaiah 45, he indicates that by exalting Christ, God emphatically declared His Son to be *Lord*, the covenant God of Israel. Everyone will reverently submit to worship this man because He is the Creator God. No one else shares the name *Lord* with the God of heaven.

*Look up the context of Isaiah 45:23 and write
down how it parallels Philippians 2:9–11.*

_____

_____

_____

_____

_____

CREATION'S CERTAIN RESPONSE

PHILIPPIANS 2:10–11

*. . . that at the name of Jesus every knee should bow,
of things in heaven, and things in earth, and things
under the earth; and that every tongue should confess that Jesus Christ is Lord, to the glory of God the
Father.*

WORD STUDY

bow—to bend; to bow; a common idiom for giving
homage

in heaven—heaven; heavenly places; referring to angels
and demons

on earth—earthly; terrestrial; referring to humans

under the earth—subterranean; referring to the dead who
will be raised

confess—to confess; to admit

glory—opinion

The final result of this exaltation will be the inevitable humility of all creation. Paul leaves us with no uncertainty. One
day, every knee will bow in worship, adoration, reverence,
and homage, recognizing Christ for His supreme power and

authority. Every tongue will verbally and publicly confess that Jesus Christ is Lord. That includes every living being in heaven, on earth, and under the earth—angels, the redeemed, men of the earth, demons, and damned souls. Imagine the majesty, pageantry, electricity, and dignity of that moment! What an atmosphere it will be! What a day! Whether saved or lost, all will be compelled to confess who Jesus Christ truly is. We can choose to worship Him as Lord and Savior either now or later. Whoever chooses the latter needs to realize that worshiping Christ is not a matter of *if* but *when* and *with what consequences.*

> *Romans 10:9 says, "That if thou shalt confess with thy mouth the Lord Jesus, and shalt believe in thine heart that God hath raised him from the dead, thou shalt be saved." What is your testimony? Have you confessed Jesus as Lord publicly? Do you believe the Father raised Him from the dead?*

And all of this is "to the glory of God the Father" (Phil. 2:11). His glad choice to super exalt Jesus to the unparalleled status of Lord may seem to detract from the Father's own glory. But the opposite is actually true. The exaltation of Christ brings glory to the Father. Jesus actually prayed for this in what is known as the High Priestly Prayer: "Father, the hour is come; glorify thy Son, that thy Son also may glorify thee" (John 17:1). And when all the universe has once again paid homage to the Son, He will also "be subject unto him that put all things under him" (1 Cor. 15:28). The Son's reign ultimately magnifies the Father.

When will the events described in Philippians 2:10–11 take place?

_____

_____

_____

_____

_____

When Paul said that "every knee should bow," why do you think he included "of things in heaven, and things in earth, and things under the earth" (Phil. 2:10)?

_____

_____

_____

_____

Explain what it means to "confess that Jesus Christ is Lord" (Phil. 2:11).

_____

_____

_____

_____

THE CHURCH'S PERFECT PATTERN

In Philippians 2:6–11 Paul has unfolded the selfless descent and glorious ascent of the incarnate God. Jesus Christ is unique, and this passage clearly accentuates His greatness. At the same time, we must also keep in mind Paul's overarching message. We should believe that what Paul has explained about Christ is true. But we should also conform our thinking to the pattern Christ has displayed. The Holy Spirit provides this illustration to encourage all believers of the value of humility and of the blessings of a humble mindset in the church.

The truth that God exalts the humble surfaces throughout Scripture. Consider the following passages.

> *The fear of the Lord is the instruction of wisdom; and before honour is humility. (Prov. 15:33)*

> *For every one that exalteth himself shall be abased; and he that humbleth himself shall be exalted. (Luke 18:14)*

> *Humble yourselves in the sight of the Lord, and he shall lift you up. (James 4:10)*

> *Yea, all of you be subject one to another, and be clothed with humility: for God resisteth the proud, and giveth grace to the humble. Humble yourselves therefore under the mighty hand of God, that he may exalt you in due time. (1 Peter 5:5–6)*

God delights to bless the humble. We can have confidence that humility is always the right choice because He always honors it. Glory came at the end of Christ's road of humble suffering (1 Pet. 1:10–11). Unity for the sake of the gospel, as well as glory in the life to come, come at the end of our road of humble service. Jesus became what we are so that we might become conformed to what He is. The result of both is exaltation.

Discuss one of the verses listed on page 60. What does it teach about humility?

_____

_____

_____

_____

_____

Do you believe that God will honor you as you humble yourself? What is one area of your life where you need to apply this belief?

_____

_____

_____

_____

RECOMMENDED READING

After spending several verses on the perfect example of Jesus Christ, Paul returns in Philippians 2:12–13 to his emphasis on living that shows the worth of the gospel. Read and review Philippians 1:27–30 as background for the next chapter of our study.

NOTES

07
HOW TO GROW SPIRITUALLY

PHILIPPIANS 2:12–13

Wherefore, my beloved, as ye have always obeyed, not as in my presence only, but now much more in my absence, work out your own salvation with fear and trembling. For it is God which worketh in you both to will and to do of his good pleasure..

Have you ever been curious about how something works? Maybe you simply googled it. Or perhaps you watched a video that inspired you to take the gadget apart and see if you could reassemble it. Have you ever thought about how a Christian grows? How does that work? In the next two verses of our study, Paul explains spiritual growth. After presenting Christ as the perfect illustration of the humble mind, the apostle returns to his original theme of *living worthy of the gospel* (Phil. 1:27) and describes what enables us to live this way. He has commanded the Philippians to stand fast in the gospel and to keep a spirit of unity within the church. Now he urges them to complete God's work in their hearts by obeying these specific commands. Obedience was the spiritual duty of the Philippian believers. Paul's heart and mind are clear on this matter. He wants them to resolve their interpersonal conflicts and to focus their energies on the progress of the gospel.

CHRIST-CENTERED MOTIVATION

The word *wherefore* indicates that Paul is applying his exhortation—explained in 1:27–2:5 and illustrated in 2:6–11—to the local situation. But what specifically is the connection between verses 12–13 and the preceding context? Though several options are possible, the closest link is between Paul's command that the Philippians obey in the present and the universal homage Christ will receive in the future. If Jesus is the exalted Lord—and He is (2:9–11)—we must live out the salvation that we claim. But there is also a link to Christ's pattern of obedience (2:8). His mindset must become ours (2:5). And this entire section has the advance of the gospel squarely in view (1:27). In other words, the motivation for sanctified Christian living comes from the redemptive work, the compelling example, and the universal sovereignty of Jesus Christ.

Paul does not distance himself from his readers. He continues with the phrase "my beloved." The apostle has already stated his love for the Philippians early in the letter: "For God is my record, how greatly I long after you all in the bowels of Jesus Christ" (1:8). He urges them with the thought that they were not merely trying to please him while he was present but were truly intent on living worthy of the gospel. He appeals to them in love to live for Christ.

> *Do you tend to be motivated by one of these three more than the others: Christ's redemptive work, Christ's compelling example, or Christ's universal sovereignty? Why do the others matter as well?*

DIVINE ENABLEMENT

PHILIPPIANS 2:13
*For it is God which worketh in you both to will and
to do of his good pleasure.*

WORD STUDY

worketh—to work; to be at work; to be active; to effect; to produce

to will—to wish; to desire; to have in mind; to purpose

to do—same root word as "worketh"

After providing Christ-centered motivation, these verses help us to get a clear understanding of how a Christian progresses in his spiritual life. There are two primary factors that contribute to spiritual growth. First, Christian maturity begins with God's working in our hearts. Paul wrote, "For it is God which worketh in you" (2:13); in other words, God energizes our spiritual desires. (The words *worketh* and *to do* translate the Greek term *energeō* from which comes the English word *energy*.) For example, picture your phone charger. Even though you can't see it, electrical current runs through the cord to recharge your phone battery. You have to recognize that your phone needs charging; the charger does not plug itself in. But the power does not come from your choice but rather from the electricity.

POWER FOR THE CHRISTIAN LIFE COMES FROM GOD.

Power for the Christian life comes from God. As Gordon Fee explains, "This verb . . . does not so much mean that God is 'doing it for [us],' but that God supplies the necessary empowering. Their obedience is ultimately something God effects in or among [us]."[1] And this divine power is related to Christ's identity as Lord. Paul prayed that the Ephesians might know "what is the exceeding greatness of his power to us-ward who believe, according to the working of his mighty power, which he wrought in Christ, when he raised him from the dead, and set him at his own right hand in the heavenly places" (Eph. 1:19–20). The power God displayed in Christ's exaltation (Phil. 2:9) is the power He demonstrates in our sanctification (Phil. 2:13).

Spiritual maturity occurs when God gives us holy desires and burdens—*to will*—to grow. Spiritual discontentment is a grace from God. He stirs us up so we'll move forward from our current spiritual state, and He enables us to accomplish—*to do*—everything He has burdened our hearts to do. God has given no commands that believers are unable to obey. God gives us both the power and the desire to fulfill His will, and as Paul had already assured the Philippians, God will complete what He has begun (Phil. 1:6).

How does God work in us to affect our desires and our practices?

---

[1] Gordon Fee, *Paul's Letter to the Philippians*, The New International Commentary on the New Testament (Grand Rapids, MI: Wm. B. Eerdmans Publishing Co., 1995), 237.

PERSONAL RESPONSIBILITY

PHILIPPIANS 2:12

*Wherefore, my beloved, as ye have always obeyed,
not as in my presence only, but now much more in
my absence, work out your own salvation with fear
and trembling.*

WORD STUDY

work out—to do; to achieve; to accomplish

salvation—an act of rescue or deliverance; preservation

fear—reverential awe for God

trembling—quivering; quaking with fear

Second, spiritual maturity also requires active, personal obedience. What does Paul mean when he said, "Work out your own salvation" (2:12)? He wasn't explaining how someone is saved from his sins. God doesn't tell us to "work *for*" our salvation, as if eternal life depends on our good works. God has already achieved our salvation. It is "of God" (1:28). In fact, "No one can work his salvation out unless God has already worked it in."[2] Therefore, Paul does not mean that we are to "work *at*" our salvation in the sense that salvation needs our work to be accomplished; rather, it has the idea of *carrying out*, such as working a longhand division problem to its intended end— the correct quotient. In Romans 7:18 Paul acknowledges that he sometimes failed to carry out God's salvation as he should.

> *For I know that nothing good dwells in me, that is,
> in my flesh; for the willing is present in me, but the
> doing [working out] of the good is not.* (NASB)

---

[2] James Montgomery Boice, *Philippians: An Expositional Commentary* (Grand Rapids, MI: Zondervan Publishing House, 1971), 162.

The key to understanding the meaning of this command is found in the phrase "as ye have always obeyed." Paul refers to what believers had been doing in the past—*obeying*—and compared their past obedience to the present—*now*. Paul was not directing his call for gospel unity to a congregation that was apathetic or apostate. The Philippians had a track record of participating in the work of the gospel (1:5), both when Paul ministered among them and after he left (2:12). But they could not be satisfied with the evidences of grace they had displayed in the past. The phrase *work out*, therefore, means to continue in obedience, bearing present fruit of eternal salvation. In chapter 2 and verse 8 Paul set before them the example of Christ, who worked out His obedience all the way to the cross. In this specific case, Paul commands believers to obey in the matter of unity and harmony: "Fulfill ye my joy, that ye be likeminded" (2:2). In other words, he told them to stop whatever squabbling was going on and to get on with being God's blameless children in pagan Philippi.

> *Scan the book of Philippians and write down ways the church had already obeyed.*

_____

_____

_____

_____

_____

> *Paul exhorts the Philippians to obey even though he was not with them. Do you struggle to please the Lord when no one is looking over your shoulder? If so, confess this to the Lord.*

_____

_____

_____

_____

_____

The truth of these two verses (Phil. 2:12–13) also illustrates the general process of spiritual growth, which always depends on our personal obedience. Sanctification is never automatic. Power for the Christian life comes from God. We should not be slow to strive for holiness through faith-filled, Spirit-empowered effort. God did not save us by our works, but He did save us "unto good works" (Eph. 2:8–10). Christian fruitfulness is the result of amazing grace. Theologian John Murray explains, "The more persistently active we are in working, the more persuaded we may be that all the energizing grace and power is of God."[3] On the other hand, the absence of spiritual progress in our lives is due to our active resistance of God's energizing power.

SCRIPTURE CONSISTENTLY HOLDS THESE TWO TRUTHS TOGETHER: GOD'S GRACE AND MAN'S RESPONSIBILITY.

The phrase "with fear and trembling" further confirms that spiritual growth is conditional. The word _fear_ describes respect for God, so that we will never want to disobey Him. The word _trembling_ conveys the idea of personal distrust in one's abilities because of the possibility of failure. It is with these attitudes that we should approach our spiritual growth, along with an urgent commitment to obedience. The mighty

_____

[3] John Murray, _Redemption: Accomplished and Applied_ (Grand Rapids: Wm. B. Eerdmans Publishing Company, 1955), 158.

acts of God in salvation and judgment should leave us awe-struck, not petrified of a vengeful God, but willing to go to any length to bring Him pleasure.

It is no coincidence, then, that the ultimate result of our growth is God's pleasure (2:13). Spiritual maturity into Christlikeness pleases the Father. He takes delight in our humble attempts to obey, feeble as they may seem. God expects and enables the reverent obedience of His people.

> *How does a believer practically* **work out** *his salvation (Phil. 2:12)? Are you taking your Christian faith for granted? What motivations does Paul give in these two verses?*

> *What is the idea behind the terms* **fear** *and* **trembling** *(Phil. 2:12)? Why is fear an important aspect of the Christian life?*

CONCLUSION

Some Christian have wondered if verses 12 and 13 contradict each other. How can you be responsible to live out your faith if it is really God who is at work? But Scripture consistently holds these two truths together: God's grace and man's responsibility. They are compatible, not contradictory. That is why throughout Paul's letters we find statements of fact about God's grace interwoven with commands that we must obey. The Christian life is all of grace, and yet we must make every effort to please the Lord.

Read the following passages which, like Philippians 2:12–13, bring together God's enablement and our responsibility—Romans 6:5–14; Ephesians 4:22–24; Colossians 3:1–5, 8–10. Write down your observations about what these verses have in common.

_____

_____

_____

_____

Explain how God helps Christians "do of his good pleasure" (Phil. 2:13).

_____

_____

_____

_____

RECOMMENDED READING

The next chapter of our study specifies how we should live worthy of the gospel as a testimony to unbelievers around us. Summarize what Peter says in 1 Peter 2:9–12 about living among a lost world.

_____

_____

_____

_____

_____

NOTES

08
SHINING LIGHTS

PHILIPPIANS 2:14–16

Do all things without murmurings and disputings: that ye may be blameless and harmless, the sons of God, without rebuke, in the midst of a crooked and perverse nation, among whom ye shine as lights in the world; holding forth the word of life; that I may rejoice in the day of Christ, that I have not run in vain, neither laboured in vain.

Sometimes when you fly at night, the altitude and cloud patterns afford a glimpse of the earth below. You can tell where towns and cities are located by the collage of lights. Without those lights, the vast space below is pitch black. The gospel of John describes the world of unbelievers as *darkness* (John 1:5; 3:19). Without God, we are desolate. But He chose to enter this world and give light (1:9). Christ is "the light of the world" (8:12), and now He has called us as His people to shine this light on the backdrop of darkness all around us (Matt. 5:14).

It is our responsibility to "work out [our] own salvation" (Phil. 2:12) in every dimension of the Christian life—our relationship with God, our private lives, and our relationships with others. In verses 14–16 Paul focuses his application on our relationships with fellow believers and the unbelieving society around us. Living worthy of the gospel means displaying an honorable testimony to the world through loving unity within the church. Let's trace Paul's teaching in these verses by considering his command, the purpose for it, and his motivation in declaring it.

PAUL'S STRONG COMMAND

PHILIPPIANS 2:14

Do all things without murmurings and disputings.

WORD STUDY

murmurings—complaint; displeasure; secret talk; whispering

disputings—reasoning; doubt; dispute

A major factor in our spiritual maturity is how we respond to life's experiences. Paul exposes two wrong responses that thwart the growth and testimony of God's children and, therefore, should be absent from our lives.

The first wrong response is murmurings. The word *murmurings* sounds like what it means—a low, sullen grumble of discontent. It describes the children of Israel when they complained about God's and Moses's leadership. On ten occasions, they chided God and contended with Him because of their challenging circumstances. (See Ex. 14:10; 15:23–24; 16:2; 17:1–2; Num. 11:1, 3–4; 14:1; 16:3–9, 29–30; 20:2–5; 21:4–6.) God reserved His severest judgment for this sin. In another letter Paul explains, "Neither let us tempt Christ, as some of them also tempted, and were destroyed of serpents. Neither murmur ye, as some of them also murmured, and were destroyed of the destroyer" (1 Cor. 10:9–10). When the Hebrews complained, in essence, they confessed that God did not and could not care for His people. They questioned His power. They suggested that His way was not perfect but was instead hard for His people, and that He made mistakes. They tested His perfect wisdom, insinuating that He was a sinner. We often direct murmuring toward other people, but this attitude reflects a stubborn, resistant unbelief in God's sovereign control.

> *What are you typically tempted to murmur about? What are your thoughts about God in these moments? Is there anything you need to confess to the Lord in response to Paul's exhortation?*

_____

_____

_____

_____

While murmurings are emotional, sinful responses to trying circumstances, *disputings* are more calculated and premeditated, involving the reasoning process. Characteristically, our discontentment toward God results in arguments with one another. When we are guilty of dissension and quarrels with one another, and when we make excuses for our unbelief and disobedience, we are questioning God's wisdom. At their root, these responses are forms of unbelief in God that undoubtedly stifle spiritual growth. The Holy Spirit is teaching us that controversy between believers is not merely interpersonal difficulty. Like murmuring, quarreling with one another evidences a wrong view of God.

LIVING FOR CHRIST IS IMPOSSIBLE WITHOUT MEDITATING ON CHRIST.

Paul positions these prohibitions after his description of Christ's exemplary humility. This order is insightful, because the apostle points us to Christ and then drives His example home. Complaining and arguing clearly do not exemplify the mind of Christ. He submitted His sinless will to the good pleasure of His Father, even though this meant death on a cross. Our Savior put the interests of others ahead of His own. Living for Christ is impossible without meditating on Christ.

What are some ways your group could help each other meditate on Christ and, thereby, avoid grumbling and arguing?

_____

_____

_____

_____

OUR EVANGELICAL WITNESS

PHILIPPIANS 2:15–16

That ye may be blameless and harmless, the sons of God, without rebuke, in the midst of a crooked and perverse nation, among whom ye shine as lights in the world; holding forth the word of life.

WORD STUDY

blameless—faultless in observable conduct; deserving no censure

harmless—pure; innocent; free from guile

sons—children

without rebuke—unblemished; blameless; cannot be censured

crooked—unscrupulous; dishonest; harsh

perverse—crooked; perverted; misled

shine—to manifest; to shine; to light up

world—the system opposed to God

holding forth—to hold fast; to hold firm; to give attention to

THE PURPOSE OF CONTENTED SUBMISSION TO GOD AND LOVING UNITY IN THE CHURCH IS THE PROMOTION OF THE GOSPEL.

Think back to Paul's imperative at the beginning of our study: "Only let your conversation be as it becometh the gospel of Christ" (1:27). The purpose of contented submission to God and loving unity in the church is the promotion of the gospel. Our obedience directly contributes to our character and influences the corrupt society in which we live. To be *blameless* means not having character deficiencies that are *handles* for others to grab hold of and discount the gospel. Our integrity—living free of blame or rebuke for sinful actions—shines like a bright light in the midst of an unscrupulous, dark generation. To be *harmless* means not mixing a Christian mindset with worldliness. Our simplicity—living with genuine and sincere motives—protects us from accusations and attacks on our testimony.

Are there any character **handles** *in your life? Are there areas in which you are mixing a Christian mindset with worldly thinking? If so, confess them to the Lord and pray for grace to forsake them.*

When we refuse to murmur and argue, we put the powerful truth of Jesus Christ on display. As a result, the community of unbelievers sees us as genuine sons of God. God chose Israel as His "peculiar treasure" to testify of His holiness as priests to the surrounding nations (Ex. 19:5–6). But the Israelites consistently failed in this mission and became "a perverse and crooked generation," just like the surrounding nations (Deut. 32:5). So God sent His Son, not only as a "covenant of the [Israelite] people" but also "a light of the Gentiles" (Isa. 42:6). And He made these believing Gentiles "an holy nation, a peculiar people" by calling us "out of darkness into his marvelous light" (1 Peter 2:9–10). Therefore, our holy living within the church demonstrates our identity as "the sons of God" and shines Christ's light to the surrounding world (Phil. 2:15). Living worthy of the gospel means letting "your light so shine before men, that they may see your good works, and glorify your Father which is in heaven" (Matt. 5:16).

*It is easy to take for granted as **normal** the mindset and habits of contemporary culture. In what ways are people on earth in today's generation "crooked and perverse"?*

One of the Israelites who lived up to his calling was Daniel. Reflect together on how Daniel exemplified the truth of Philippians 2:15. How can you apply these lessons in your own life?

_____

_____

_____

_____

Paul then describes the key to living as God's children—
"holding [fast] the word of life" (2:16). As believers strongly
grip this gospel in their lives, its life-giving power works in
the hearts of unbelievers. This series of effects is why Paul was
so concerned about the way the believers live. Our character
flows from the life-giving gospel and, in turn, directly impacts
its reception and progress in our community. Paul emphasizes
personal holiness in all his epistles, but it is not an isolated
goal. As Handley Moule observes, "A passage like this shews
us how entirely [the apostles] take it for granted all the time
that the Churches would never concentrate themselves upon
merely their own Christian life."[1]

> *What does "shin[ing] as lights in the world"*
> *(Phil. 2:15) have to do with the gospel?*

_____

_____

_____

_____

_____

[1] H. C. G. Moule, *Philippian Studies: Lessons in Faith and Love from
St. Paul's Epistle to the Philippians* (London: Hodder and Stoughton, 1904),
126.

AN ETERNAL PERSPECTIVE

PHILIPPIANS 2:16

*. . . that I may rejoice in the day of Christ, that I
have not run in vain, neither laboured in vain.*

WORD STUDY

rejoice—boast; glory

day of Christ—second coming of Christ; day Christ will
return from heaven

run—to strive to advance; to make progress

vain—empty; without content; without result

labored—worked hard; struggled; labored to the point of
exhaustion

In the end Paul had an eschatological vision in which he stood
before Christ in the judgment. Paul does not mean "on the day
of Christ" but rather "with the day of Christ in view."[2] He fore-
saw the potential joy of that momentous event. His hope was
that the race he had run and the work he had done would have
eternal significance. His ability to boast, however, depended
on the Philippians' faithfulness. Paul's ministry was effective
to the degree they heeded his message.

Paul's motivation of boasting is not arrogance. The apostle is
not bragging about his own accomplishments. Rather, he is
communicating a passionate concern that the gospel run its
course in the Philippians' lives. He understands that profes-
sions of faith that do not culminate in living worthy of the

---

[2] Gordon D. Fee, *Paul's Letter to the Philippians*, The New International Commentary on the New Testament (Grand Rapids: Eerdmans, 1995),
248n40.

gospel are empty. They leave those who minister the truth like Paul with nothing to present to Christ for His eternal glory.

There is no question whether or not "every tongue [will] confess that Jesus Christ is Lord" (2:11). There is no question whether God who has "begun a good work in you will perform it until the day of Jesus Christ" (1:6). But your sincere effort to "work out your own salvation" is a matter that necessitates faith-filled "fear and trembling" (2:12). Paul had an eternal perspective on the importance of displaying an honorable testimony to the world through loving, gospel-focused unity within the church, and so must we.

Who has labored in Christ to give you the gospel and help you grow in it? How should their reason for boasting in the Lord on Judgment Day motivate you?

_____

_____

_____

_____

_____

Why do we often struggle to maintain an eternal perspective on our obedience to Christ? What would help us keep eternity in view?

_____

_____

_____

_____

RECOMMENDED READING

For another look at how Paul personally applied a gospel focus, read 1 Corinthians 9:19–27. How did Paul *run* "for the gospel's sake" (9:23)?

_____

_____

_____

_____

_____

NOTES

09
JOYFUL SACRIFICE

PHILIPPIANS 2:17–18

Yea, and if I be offered upon the sacrifice and service of your faith, I joy, and rejoice with you all. For the same cause also do ye joy, and rejoice with me.

Have you ever known a Christian who maintained a joyful spirit in the face difficult circumstances? Perhaps this was someone who encouraged fellow believers who were struggling in spite of his own diagnosis of terminal cancer. Maybe it was a widow who ministered to grieving family members and friends in the midst of her own sorrow. God gives grace so that His people can rejoice even when assaulted by trials at every turn, because we know God is maturing us (James 1:2–4) and that He orchestrates everything for our good and His Son's glory (Rom. 8:28–29).

SPIRITUAL JOY FINDS ITS SOURCE IN THE LORD AND ITS SUBSTANCE IN THE GOSPEL.

One of the most striking accounts of joy in all Scripture is Paul and Silas praying to and praising God in the deep recesses of the Philippian jail (Acts 16:25). Luke's account of this prison praise service provides a window into the apostle's mindset of finding joy in God while sacrificing to proclaim His gospel. Paul concludes the passage we have been studying with a manifestation of his sacrificial love for the Philippians and a demonstration of the pathway to true joy.

AN APOSTOLIC PATTERN OF JOY

Throughout Philippians, we see Paul as the Christlike model of joyful Christian maturity. He projects his personal joy as a motive for their obedience: "Fulfil ye my joy" (Phil. 2:2) and "Rejoice with me" (2:18). This is not a selfish plea but a paradigm of true joy. Sixteen times in this letter Paul addresses the lofty subject of the believer's joy. This sublime quality was the driving desire of the apostle's life. Spiritual joy finds its source in the Lord and its substance in the gospel—His saving work in the lives of people. That's why Paul's joy was deeply affected by the Philippians' response to this epistle as they lived worthy of the gospel and progressed in their spiritual maturity.

Let's survey the passages in Philippians that mention *joy*.

JOY PASSAGES IN PHILIPPIANS
(emphasis added)

Always in every prayer of mine for you all making request with **joy.** *(1:4)*

What then? notwithstanding, every way, whether in pretence, or in truth, Christ is preached; and I therein do **rejoice,** *yea, and will* **rejoice.** *(1:18)*

And having this confidence, I know that I shall abide and continue with you all for your furtherance and **joy** *of faith. (1:25)*

That your **rejoicing** *may be more abundant in Jesus Christ for me by my coming to you again. (1:26)*

*Fulfil ye my **joy**, that ye be likeminded, having the same love, being of one accord, of one mind. (2:2)*

*Yea, and if I be offered upon the sacrifice and service of your faith, I **joy**, and **rejoice** with you all. (2:17)*

*For the same cause also do ye **joy**, and **rejoice** with me. (2:18)*

*I sent him therefore the more carefully, that, when ye see him again, ye may **rejoice**, and that I may be the less sorrowful. (2:28)*

*Receive him therefore in the Lord with all **gladness**; and hold such in reputation. (2:29)*

*Finally, my brethren, **rejoice** in the Lord. To write the same things to you, to me indeed is not grievous, but for you it is safe. (3:1)*

*Therefore, my brethren dearly beloved and longed for, my **joy** and crown, so stand fast in the Lord, my dearly beloved. (4:1)*

***Rejoice** in the Lord alway: and again I say, **Rejoice**. (4:4)*

*In which four verses above does Paul either combine **joy** and **rejoice** or repeat **rejoice**? Why do you think he does this?*

_____

_____

_____

_____

_____

Who or what does Paul indicate is the source of his joy? In what circumstances is he rejoicing or exhorting his readers to rejoice? What can we learn from his example?

_____

_____

_____

_____

DELIGHT IN GOD IS THE FRUIT OF REGENERATION.

Joy is an act of faith and surrender to God. We choose to turn from the temporary lusts and pleasures of this world and to look to the Lord alone as our chief Source of delight. The natural, unredeemed person has no capacity to see the invisible, spiritual world of faith. Only believers can see the unseen! That's what faith is (Heb. 11:1). We have a new heart that was implanted by the sovereign work of the Holy Spirit. The result is a new love for God poured into our souls. Delight in God is the fruit of regeneration. Through diligent study of Scripture, the Spirit of God progressively transforms our minds, and our delight in God increases.

Are you a joyful Christian? Is there something or someone you are allowing to obstruct your joy? Do you find yourself meditating on Scripture in a way that cultivates joy in your heart? Is there something you should change in light of the emphasis in Philippians on joy?

_____

_____

A MUTUALLY SACRIFICIAL OFFERING

PHILIPPIANS 2:17

*Yea, and if I be offered upon the sacrifice and service
of your faith, I joy, and rejoice with you all.*

WORD STUDY

offered—to be poured out as a drink offering

sacrifice—an act of offering

service—ceremonial duty; ministry

rejoice—to rejoice together with; take part in another's joy

With spiritual joy in mind, Paul was willing to make whatever sacrifice was necessary for the benefit and blessing of the church. He describes his life metaphorically as a sacrifice offered in the temple during the service of the priesthood. Part of this ritual involved the pouring of a drink offering over a burnt offering that was being consumed by the altar's fire. Paul visualized the faith of the Philippians as an ancient sacrifice during the ritual service of the priesthood. Like every other church, they were not perfect. He expresses concern about disunity in their midst and the false teaching that could corrupt their Christianity as it has in so many congregations. He also admonished them not to be anxious. However, Paul unreservedly commends the Philippians as faithful believers. In fact, one of his reasons for joy was their "fellowship in the gospel from the first day until now" (1:5).

In particular, this church had faithfully supported Paul ever since the Lord miraculously established a congregation in this pagan Roman colony. Now, with the gift that prompted Paul's letter, the Philippian church had raised their support to a new level. It was no small act of loving sacrifice to send Epaphroditus eight hundred miles to "supply [the Philippians'] lack of service toward [Paul]" (2:30). This "lack of service" initially sounds like they were lackluster in their ministry to Paul. What he means, however, is that the missing element of their ministry was not having a recent opportunity to support Paul in person, a void admirably filled by Epaphroditus. Paul extols this messenger for living worthy of the gospel: "Because for the work of Christ he was nigh unto death, not regarding his life" (2:30). His journey of faith, compelled by his church's concern for Paul, was "a sacrifice acceptable, wellpleasing to God" (4:18). The Philippians were doing what Paul commands in Romans: "present your bodies a living sacrifice, holy, acceptable unto God, which is your reasonable service" (Rom. 12:1).

What is the basis of Paul's appeal in Romans 12:1 to present ourselves as living sacrifices? What are some of God's mercies that you need to keep in view?

_____

_____

_____

_____

Can you look back over the past month and point to ways you have poured yourself out for the spiritual well-being of others? Have you been able to do this with joy? What truth from this chapter could God use to motivate and enable you to sacrificially minister during the next month?

_____

_____

_____

_____

_____

Like a burnt offering, the Philippians had rendered "the sacrifice and service of [their] faith" (Phil. 2:17). Paul viewed his life like a drink offering being poured onto the Philippians' faith. He willingly and joyfully gave his life, even in death, for the benefit of the believers' faith. Though the verb translated "be offered" does not denote "being killed," it can refer to a martyr's death. (See 2 Timothy 4:6.) This seems to be Paul's meaning, even though he does not mean a martyr's death is inevitable or immediate. There is strong evidence in this letter that Paul thought he would be set free. Nevertheless, he had spent his life for the sake of the gospel and, therefore, for the sake of God's people. Eventually, this way of life would mean death. But what price is too high to pay for a Savior who submitted Himself to death on a cross? Why wouldn't Paul pour out his life to declare the good news of a Savior who emptied Himself to become a servant (Phil. 2:7)?

> *How far was Paul willing to go in order to achieve his goal? How far will each of us go to help our friends grow in the Lord? Does Paul's example sound too radical? Why or why not?*

_____

_____

_____

_____

As he joyfully chose to make this sacrifice, Paul urges the Philippians to rejoice in like manner for the same purpose. His repetition of *joy* and *rejoice* in verses 17 and 18 emphasizes the importance of joy as well as his union with the Philippians. As we involve our lives in God's purpose and work in the world, we soon find fresh, new joy in serving others and in advancing the gospel. There *is* joy in serving Jesus! Paul's sacrificial life became the supreme model of joy for the whole church, and he urged all believers to choose the same lifestyle.

> *How did Paul want the church to respond to his sacrifice? What does this indicate about the mindset of a true servant of God?*

_____

_____

_____

_____

_____

RECOMMENDED READING

The final chapter of this study reviews Paul's message in Philippians 1:27–2:18. Take a few moments to read the passage one more time and reflect on what God has taught you through it.

NOTES

10
LIVING AS A
HEAVENLY CITIZEN

We began our study with an overview of the book of Philippians. Let's conclude it by reviewing the overarching truth of 1:27–2:18. Like a flag that the soldiers carry out to raise and fly proudly atop their pole, this passage unfolds from a compact but potent command: "Only let your conversation be as it becometh the gospel of Christ" (1:27). This call to live worthy of the gospel—or to live as citizens of heaven—orients us to the message of these twenty-two verses.

THE RESPONSIBILITIES OF
HEAVENLY CITIZENSHIP

All of us enjoy the privileges of citizenship. Some are blessed with the benefits of dual citizenship, which makes travel and options for residence much simpler. However, as the proverbial saying goes, *with privilege comes responsibility*. National governments have established laws for their citizens. And in most countries there are cultural expectations inherent in being a citizen, such as respecting the flag and affirming the pledge. As diverse as the United States of America is, the national anthem is still played or sung at the beginning of many major events. Professional athletes, who often seem solely bent on individual glory, band together to represent their country at the Olympics. They accept the responsibility of a citizen to proudly display their country's colors in competition.

Paul makes use of this metaphor in his letter to the Philippians. They enjoyed certain rights as citizens of a Roman colony. But their most important citizenship had nothing to do with Rome or property ownership or anthems and flags. He emphatically states, "Our conversation [i.e., citizenship] is in heaven," because that is where the Savior reigns (3:20). Since this is the case, it was imperative that they behaved like heavenly citizens, living in a way that displayed the worth of the gospel (1:27). This is our duty as well.

The exhortation to walk worthy of our heavenly citizenship is parallel to what Paul says in Ephesians 4:1: "I therefore, the prisoner of the Lord, beseech you that ye walk worthy of the vocation wherewith ye are called." We cannot do enough good to merit heaven. Living worthy of the gospel does not mean earning the grace of the gospel. But just as there are responsibilities of being a citizen of Singapore or another country, there are also responsibilities of being a citizen of heaven—living for the sake of the gospel, giving our ultimate loyalty to the Lord Jesus Christ, and learning to "observe all things whatsoever [Christ has] commanded you" (Matt. 28:20).

What are some of the challenges of having dual citizenship in both an earthly country and the kingdom of heaven? How can we appropriately honor our country but live out the reality that our ultimate citizenship is in heaven?

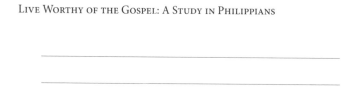

THE PATHWAY OF HEAVENLY CITIZENSHIP

In nineteenth-century America, laborers worked feverishly to lay railroad tracks across huge stretches of undeveloped territory. One track necessarily led to the next. In our passage of study Paul has likewise laid down a succession of truths to help us understand what living worthy of the gospel looks like. Each piece of truth Paul presents is important in and of itself. But it also inevitably leads to another truth or responsibility.

Striving Together for the Gospel's Sake

The passage begins with a command to exercise our heavenly citizenship by courageously proclaiming the gospel in spite of persecution. Being a citizen of heaven does not mean standing still but standing strong. In order to "[strive] together for the faith of the gospel" we must maintain unity in that gospel, as indicated by phrases such as "one spirit" and "one mind" (1:27; 2:2). This pursuit of unity is not based simply on being nice or on reducing the faith to the lowest common denominator so that everyone is satisfied. There are blessings we enjoy together in the Spirit that provide the motivation and ability to live in unity for the gospel's sake (2:1). And the heart of this unity is "having the same love" for Christ and one another (2:2).

Pursuing Unity Through Humility

Unity is of utmost importance, because the mission God has given the church to make disciples of all nations is severely impeded when we prioritize by our own desires and agendas. Therefore, Paul next emphasizes that spiritual unity requires a spirit of humility. *Like-mindedness* is *low-mindedness*. Living worthy of the gospel is not insisting on our own way or pursuing our own ambitions but placing the value of others ahead of our own (2:3) and giving careful attention to others' needs, not just our own (2:4).

> *How can we exhibit humility toward other believers with whom we disagree? Does this mean we should not have strong convictions?*

> *Have you noticed a difference in your outlook since you studied these verses several weeks ago? Why or why not? What is one specific area of humility you want to give more prayerful attention?*

Becoming Conformed to the Mindset of Christ

After exhorting us to pursue unity through humility, Paul provides the most powerful pattern imaginable in the self-chosen humiliation of Christ Jesus. Gospel-worthy humility is impossible unless we meditate on Christ and are conformed to His mindset (2:5).

He set aside the privileges of deity and came to earth "in the likeness of men," willingly giving rather than grasping (2:6). He retained "the form of God" but added to it "the form of a servant" (2:7). The final aspect of this exemplary mindset is the Son's humble obedience to the Father's will, which led Christ all the way down to the cross (2:8). Although the exact actions of Christ's humility are for us as sinners unrepeatable and unreachable, His humble mindset lies at the heart of the image into which God is conforming His people (Rom. 8:29).

In what ways is Jesus' humble sacrifice unrepeatable? In what ways is it a mindset you must adopt? What would that look like this week?

_____

_____

_____

_____

Understanding the Path to Exaltation

JESUS BECAME WHAT WE ARE SO THAT WE MIGHT BECOME CONFORMED TO WHAT HE IS.

Paul's portrayal of Christ does not end on a low note. Because Christ selflessly chose to lower Himself, His Father gladly chose to exalt Him (2:9). There is no longer any mistaking the identity and position of Jesus Christ. He has the greatest name possible. He is the Lord, and one day all of creation will humbly acknowledge this (2:10–11). Christ's incarnate life is the supreme testimony to God's consistent practice of exalting the humble. We can have confidence that God will honor our self-emptying humility. Jesus became what we are so that we might become conformed to what He is. The result of both is exaltation.

Persevering by the Grace of God

The sacrificial life and universal lordship of Jesus Christ provides compelling motivation to persevere in living worthy of the gospel. After illustrating the humble path to glory, Paul explains the two sides of spiritual growth. Living worthy of the gospel in the likeness of Christ entails both human responsibility and divine enablement. God has promised to complete in us His sanctifying work (1:6). The result is certain. But He has also ordained our faith-filled obedience to His Word as the means by which we progressively grow in sanctification. Consequently, Paul weaves together a command to "work out our salvation" (2:12) with an assurance that God is right now giving us the desire and ability to do so (2:13).

> *It is easy to veer toward one ditch or the other. Either we work and rely on our own strength and glory in our own accomplishments, or we mistake grace for license to do what we want or an excuse not to put forth much effort at all. How can we avoid these ditches in everyday life this week?*

_____

_____

_____

_____

_____

Shining As Lights in the World

The passage then moves from a general exhortation to persevere by God's grace to a specific imperative not to complain and argue (2:14). Disunity was one of the problems in the Philippian church and, therefore, receives Paul's special focus in knowing what it means to live worthy of the gospel. In this section we learn that the significance of our obedience goes well beyond our personal lives and even our relationships with other believers. Holiness and love within the church brightly beam the gospel to the lost world around the church (2:15). By maintaining an eternal perspective, we have more than enough motivation to tightly grasp the gospel and see God spread its life-giving power (2:16).

Finding Joy Through Sacrifice

Paul concludes this passage by affirming his joy and commending it to his readers. The pathway to spiritual maturity requires sacrifice for all of us, not just apostles. But there is joy in laying everything on the altar for the sake of the gospel (2:17). The Philippians had demonstrated remarkable commitment to Paul and his gospel ministry. He wanted them to continue with the confidence that no amount of adversity can quench the joy that arises through gospel-focused living (2:18).

Take one of the sections of this study and share a testimony of how God has used it to renew your mind.

THE ESSENCE OF HEAVENLY CITIZENSHIP

One final aspect of Paul's letter merits attention as we complete this study. Though this epistle is more autobiographical than most of Paul's inspired correspondence, the apostle himself is not the central figure. Sterling examples like Timothy and Epaphroditus are important but secondary as well. And though Paul wrote to the Philippians with their current circumstances clearly in view, their lives are not the main point of the letter either. As twenty-first-century readers we need to apply this divinely inspired teaching personally and collectively. But we cannot do so by focusing on ourselves.

The most important person in Philippians is Jesus Christ. Paul captures this reality in one

WE LIVE WORTHY OF THE GOSPEL BY FOCUSING ON HIM.

potent declaration, "To live is Christ" (1:21). We live worthy of the gospel by focusing on Him. The centrality of Christ permeates this letter in numerous ways. For example, Paul uses phrases such as "in Christ" and "in the Lord" nearly twenty times. The second coming of Christ serves as a primary motivation in several passages (1:6, 10; 2:10–11, 16; 3:20–21). More than anything else, Paul wanted to know Christ (3:10). He had lived a highly respectable religious life before his conversion. If anyone had reason to glory in his status and accomplishments, it was Paul. However, he not only left all this behind but considered it waste in comparison to being "found in [Christ]" (3:9).

In the economy of heaven, which is the one that really matters, to gain Christ is to gain everything (3:8). Our Savior is the essence of heavenly citizenship.

> *Read through Philippians with a colored pencil (or electronic markup tool) in hand. Highlight every reference to Jesus Christ. Scan through these references and meditate on what Paul means by saying, "to live is Christ."*

_____

_____

_____

_____

CONCLUSION

We have had the privilege of studying a rich portion of Scripture that in many ways captures the essence of the Christian life. It's a stretch of "spiritual railroad" that we need to review often. And we can do so with the guarantee that God is energizing even the feeblest of faith-filled efforts to live worthy of the gospel. With minds fixed on Jesus Christ, we can follow the example of Paul in spiritually mature living that is full of joy.

NOTES